The Pursuit of Purpose

How To Discover God's Will For Your Life

By

Clarence L. Haynes Jr.

ISBN: 9781096699347

Front cover image by Diana N. Haynes

Book design by Diana N. Haynes

Graphic design by Lidia Corey
www.sanddragonmedia.com

Clarence L. Haynes Jr.
42 Lake Ave Ext., #138
Danbury, CT 06811

This book was published with the encouragement and free support of members of The Bible Study Club:

www.thebiblestudyclub.com

Acknowledgements

Thank you to everyone who encouraged me to pursue writing and to everyone who played a role in motivating and helping me regardless of how big or small it was. Thanks to my wife Diana for being my partner in life and in ministry.

Contents

Foreword

We all go through life looking for meaning and fulfillment. We all want answers to the big questions, like why am I here and what mark am I meant to leave on this world? Those who find the answer to those questions discover that meaning and fulfillment we are all looking for.

The quest for these answers is attested to by the volumes of books written on discovering one's purpose and their success. Consequently, when Clarence shared his book with me, I assumed the contents would be a regurgitation of what's already been said. I was surprisingly wrong. In his own unique way, Clarence gives both the average Joe and the successful entrepreneur the practical ways anyone can discover their personal why and experience the magic and momentum of leading the life they have been purposed for. As you read through the pages of this book you will be inspired and empowered to grab hold of your God-given purpose and unlock the life you were meant to live!

Frank Santora

Lead Pastor of Faith Church

www.faithchurch.cc

Introduction

Thank you for taking the time to read this book. I want you to know this book is written as a conversation between friends. As you read the pages imagine you and I were sitting down in a Starbucks having a chat over a cup of coffee (hot chocolate for me) talking about this subject. I have written each page with that in mind, and I pray that comes through as you read the pages of this book.

Many great conversations begin with a question, and I want to ask you one. Why are you here? No, not why are you reading this book or why are you having this conversation but why are you here? Why were you created to live in this country, in this city, in this family, in this arena, at this time? I will tell you why. Because God has a purpose and plan for you that is necessary for the day and age in which you live. Here is a reminder from Ephesians -

"For we are God's masterpiece. He has created us anew in Christ Jesus, so we can do the good things he planned for us long ago." (Ephesians 2:10 NLT)

Let's personalize this:

For *you* are God's masterpiece. He has created *you* anew in Christ Jesus, so *you* can do the good things he planned for *you* long ago.

Most if not all Christians understand that and hopefully believe that. I am sure you do, or you wouldn't be reading a book like this. However, once you do realize that, now what?

How do you take this belief and transfer that into knowing what that purpose and plan is? This is a question that cannot go unanswered and a yearning that won't be quenched until you figure it out.

For this reason, I am glad you are here today and that you have chosen to take this journey with me. By the time we have finished our conversation, it is possible you may have discovered your purpose. If you have, we will praise God for that. The more likely scenario is that by the time we have finished our conversation you will have a greater understanding of God's will and purpose for you. You will also discover the different ways God leads you into it. In other words, you will know what to look for. This understanding will ultimately lead you into the plan God has for you. Simply put, our conversation is about putting you on the right path and steering you in the right direction.

Consider this your road map.

It is not just about getting to the destination but building a foundation that will allow you to understand how you got there. Whether you realize it or not this question of God's will for you is one that will be considered many times in your life's journey. It will continually be asked and will need to be answered at various stages as you progress through life. That's why it is critical not just to know God's purpose (the destination); it is vital to understand how he leads you into it (the journey).

If you want to know the "what" and the "how" so you can navigate through life. If you want to understand and fulfill the incredible plan God has for you. Then I am happy that you are here. You are in the right place. Pull up a chair and snuggle in. Grab your coffee or hot chocolate and let's get on with this pursuit of purpose.

Chapter 1 -
God, What Is Your Will for My Life?

When you look in the dictionary the word purpose is defined as follows - the reason for which something is done or created or for which something exists.

In preparing to write this I did a search on google for "how to find your purpose." This search turned up 1.8 billion results. This search let me know that there are a lot of people looking. It also means there are lots of answers out there. However, just because there is a lot of information that does not make discovering your purpose any easier.

As Christians on this journey trying to discover why you are here (your purpose), this inevitably will lead you to ask the question

"God, what is your will for my life?"

This is true of anyone seeking to be a faithful follower of Christ.

As a Christian, I believe you can't have a conversation about your purpose without connecting it to God's will.

Once you have asked the question the challenge becomes how to demystify, and decipher what God really wants you to do. At the center of the challenge is the fact that people often approach this in a very narrow way. I believe this happens because people typically approach this topic from a strictly spiritual perspective. Please do not misunderstand, finding God's will and purpose is a spiritual discipline. However, I have discovered that the way God reveals this to you is not just by spiritual means he also uses practical ones as well.

As we begin to travel down this road of discovery, I want to introduce to you and help you understand some different aspects of God's will. There are three aspects to God's will I want to highlight that apply to every believer:

God's general will

God's specific will

God's daily will

Let's look at each one individually.

God's general will

God's general will applies to you if you are a Christian. It doesn't matter how old you are, where you live, what you do, married or single. If you are a believer in Jesus Christ, then this applies to you. Let me give you some examples:

"Therefore, go and make disciples of all the nations, baptizing them in the name of the Father and the Son and the Holy Spirit. Teach these new disciples to obey all the commands I have given you. And be sure of this: I am with you always, even to the end of the age." (Matthew 28:19-20 NLT)

This verse is known as the Great Commission which applies to every Christian. It is God's will that we would preach or share the gospel and make disciples of all nations. We are all responsible for doing this. Some have larger platforms to accomplish this task, but it applies to every believer.

Here is another one:

"Be thankful in all circumstances, **for this is God's will for you** *who belong to Christ Jesus." (1 Thessalonians 5:18 NLT, emphasis added)*

Again, this is something that applies to every believer. If you belong to Christ Jesus then God's will for you is that you will be thankful in all circumstances.

When it comes to God's general will, it is relatively easy to understand. You don't have to question what God is asking you to do. God's general will is plain and clear. You will find it written within the pages of scripture, and it is pretty much black and white. Whether you obey it or not is another story. However, I am confident in saying that discovering God's general will is not the source of your struggle. As long as you are reading the Bible, you will discover God's general will for your life. You may struggle in doing it, but you won't struggle in knowing it.

Of the different aspects of God's will, this one is probably the easiest to understand.

The confusion and challenges begin to increase when we examine the next element of God's will.

God's specific will

God's specific will, unfortunately, is not black and white. It encompasses many different shades of grey, probably way more than fifty. God's specific will includes things like,

Your occupation – What job should you seek?
Your vocation – What career path should you go down?
Your ministry – Where do you serve?
Part-time or Full time?
Marriage – Should you get married and if yes to whom?
Where should you live?
Which college should you choose?
What do you do with the rest of your life?
You are about to retire, now what?
What church should you attend?
Do you leave your church or stay where you are?
Should you change careers or stay in your current one?

These may be the types of questions you are asking. You are possibly searching for answers, if not to these specific questions, then to ones similar to them.

The challenge in uncovering God's specific will is that there is not a particular scripture you can turn to that will give you the answer to many of these questions. Can you find a scripture that says thus saith the Lord, this is the job you should have? It doesn't exist. So, what do you do?

For these scenarios, you can still turn to scripture. Scripture will supply the guidelines by how you go about making these decisions and finding answers. For example:

> *"Trust in the LORD with all your heart; Do not depend on your own understanding. Seek his will in all you do, and he will show you which path to take." (Proverbs 3:5-6 NLT)*

> *"Without wise leadership, a nation falls; there is safety in having many advisers."*

(Proverbs 11:14 - NLT)

"And I will ask the Father, and he will give you another Advocate, who will never leave you. He is the Holy Spirit, who leads into all truth…"
(John 14:16-17a NLT)

"For all who are led by the Spirit of God are children of God." (Romans 8:14 NLT)

I hope you are beginning to see how the guidelines work when it comes to discovering God's specific will.

The Guidelines:

> Trust God not your own understanding.
>
> Seek God.
>
> Get counsel and advice.
>
> Be led by the Holy Spirit.

God's specific will is born out of your relationship with him. You cannot discover his plan apart from him. God's specific will is something you are led into, and it flows out of your relationship with him. With that in mind here are some things to consider.

Are you spending time in prayer? - Jesus said my sheep hear me and know my voice

Are you spending time in worship? – Becoming familiar with God's presence

Are you spending time in silence? – Listening to what God is saying to your heart

Are you spending time in the Word? – God will not ask you to do something contrary to his word

You cannot find and discover God's specific will without spending time with him. It won't happen. Let me repeat that. You cannot find God's specific will without spending time with him. Spending time with him sets the stage and allows him to reveal to you what direction he wants you to go. There is no other way to get to his specific will. The good news is that scripture uncovers many of the ways God leads you into his will and how he reveals his plan to you. If you keep reading, I am going to disclose those to you in just a little while but don't jump ahead yet because we have to look at one more aspect of God's will.

God's Daily Will

The third aspect of God's will to consider is his daily will. What is it that you want me to do today? If you want to be technical, God's specific will is the culmination of you consistently following

God's daily will. His daily will consists of the choices, decisions, and actions you take on a day to day basis. Here are some examples of God's daily will in action:

You feel compelled to call someone out of the blue, do you do it or not?

You feel the need to take a different direction home today, do you follow the leading?

You are in conversation with someone, and you feel led to share the gospel with that person, do you do it?

You feel the need to pray for a person at a specific moment.

You have a family situation that requires a response, and you ask God what do you want me to do?

You are on the job, and you have a decision to make, so you ask God what to do.

Recently a friend of mine that I grew up with passed away. He had been dealing with some health challenges for a while. At his funeral, they shared this story.

A few months before his passing he was visiting his mom. His mom had cooked some good food, so he decided to delay his return flight back home to stay with mom and enjoy the food. Who doesn't like mom's home cooking?

A little while later he felt in his heart that he couldn't stay at his mom's house but had to leave. He didn't understand why but he knew God was leading him to return home. The next day he got on a flight to return home and while on the plane there was a passenger who was having a heart attack. The flight attendants were looking for a doctor on the flight, but there wasn't one.

As the flight attendant was passing by in the aisle, my friend asked what the problem was, and they told him. My friend wasn't a doctor, but he had some heart issues and was traveling with his medication, nitroglycerin, which would be able to help this gentleman in distress. He gave it to the flight attendant with some instructions on how to use it. This medication was able to help the man until they were able to land the plane and get this passenger the proper medical attention. In this instance, his obedience to God's daily will put him in a position where he helped save someone else's life.

There are numerous types of scenarios that require immediate decisions or choices, and you need God's immediate direction to make the right choice. There are also many times the Holy Spirit will want to direct your actions. The question is will you listen and obey? These are all part of God's daily will and like his specific will are born out of your relationship with God, being led by the Holy Spirit and guided by scripture.

I will also add there are some choices that God will allow you to make without much interference. If you remember in the Garden of Eden, God said you can eat from any tree in the garden, except one. He gave them a guideline, and he didn't worry about whether they ate a banana one day, a peach the next, maybe a pear the following day.

God will give you guidelines and the freedom to move around within those guidelines. So yes, you can determine where you want to go on vacation, what restaurant you want to eat in and other decisions like these because God gives you the freedom to choose. There will be times when God will interrupt your plan and compel you to move in a specific direction even in these "simpler" matters. For the most part, however, He allows you to decide.

One more thing about our Heavenly Father. If you ask for his help, even in these "simpler" areas, he will give it because he cares about you.

"Give all your worries and cares to God, for he cares about you." (1 Peter 5:7 NLT)

There is nothing too small that you can't consult your Heavenly Father on.

God's daily will is merely understanding that even in your day to day choices God has a plan for them. Just like the specific will if you will spend time in fellowship with him, he will direct your paths and show you what you need to do.

After looking at these three aspects of God's will, you are probably saying, how does that get me closer to understanding and fulfilling God's purpose?

We are now going to look at different ways God has used, and continues to use, to lead people like you and me into his purpose. I am going to reveal to you eleven different ways God can lead you into his will and his divine purpose for your life. None of this is mystical, in fact, it is very practical, and they all come from within the guidelines and pages of scripture.

I remember when I was a teenager, and I was seeking and asking God to show me his will and purpose for my life. I was waiting for my grand revelation. I was waiting for the heavens to open and the voice declaring "Clarence, this is the direction I want you to walk in."

As you can imagine, that never happened. I'm not saying it can't, but it didn't happen to me. I have since discovered over time that for the overwhelming majority of us, God's revelation is not going to come that way. We have to learn not to look for the earthquake, or the fire but to listen for the still small voice. The chances are that is how God is going to lead you and reveal his purpose to you.

Now on to the first of the eleven ways.

Chapter 2 -
Go, and I Will Show

"The Lord had said to Abram, "Go from your country, your people and your father's household to the land I will show you."
(Genesis 12:1 - NIV)

I n this portion of scripture, we see God giving Abraham a command. Leave where you are, take your wife and servants with you and go to a land that I will show you. For a moment I want you to put yourself in Abrahams's shoes. Imagine Abraham going to Sarah and saying "hey honey we are leaving. Where are we going? I have no idea but pack up everything because we are not coming back."

Does that sound a little crazy? Do you think you could get your spouse to go for that one?

In fact, in today's church world if you came to your pastor and said I am packing up everything, selling my house, leaving my job and moving. I don't know where I'm going, but this is what God told me to do. He may look at you like you are crazy and everyone around you will probably do the same thing, including your family.

The bible doesn't record Sarah's immediate response, but I wonder if she thought her husband was crazy.

However, sometimes when God is leading you, there may be no clear indication of where you are going or what you must do. All you have is a sense that you must go. You get a nudge or urge or a leading that it's time to move. I am not saying you should respond like this to every leading or impulse. However, you can't discount these because this could be God's way of getting you to move.

The beauty of Abraham's story is that he didn't need faith for the whole journey. He just needed enough faith to be willing to take the first step. Go, and I will show is about one thing, will you trust God enough to take the first step in the direction that he is leading you?

That's why a relationship and spending time with God to fine tune your ear to his voice is so crucial. It is also why you cannot discover God's purpose outside of this relationship.

There are challenges when God is leading you in this fashion. The first one is internal. God, is that really you? Did I hear you correctly? This is an internal struggle you face not because you want to be disobedient, even though that may be true for some. This struggle comes because you want to be clear you are hearing God's voice and direction. The goal is making sure it is his voice and not some other one, including your own, that you are following. The one thing that is critical, if you are going to move in a leading like this...you must be sure of God's voice.

The other challenge in this type of leading is external. When God is leading you like this, it is difficult to justify to those around you (not that you always have to). All you are moving on is a command (Go) and a promise (I will show). In Abraham's life, God didn't give the command to Sarah. He gave it to Abraham. Sarah had to trust that her husband was hearing from God. In this type of leading God may be speaking to just you or just you and your spouse. You may not get support from those around you, and that's why you have to be clear you are following God's voice.

I met Diana in September of 2011. After about two weeks of dating, I knew she was the one I was going to marry. I distinctly remember one Sunday sitting around the dinner table with my family; it was in early October. God spoke to my heart about our relationship and said one word...ordained. He was telling me that he ordained this relationship. By December of 2011 just three months after we met, we were married.

Many people thought we were crazy, and we were moving too fast. But I know that I had heard an explicit confirmation in my heart from God, that no one else had heard. This confirmation gave me the confidence to move forward. By the way at the time of this writing, we are now celebrating seven years of marriage.

You don't need faith for the whole journey, just be willing to take the first step.

When God is leading you with Go, and I will show, this is how it could be. You may have to tune out the voices around you and move in the confidence that you have heard from God. Everyone may not support you or even understand you. However, if you are confident you have heard from God, and that is the crux, then you have to move in what he has told you to do.

Don't worry everyone else will eventually catch up. Remember you don't need faith for the whole journey, just be willing to take the first step.

Questions to consider:

Is there something in your heart that you specifically feel like God is telling you to do?

Does it feel a little unclear because you don't know all the steps?

Practical application: Write down exactly what you believe God is telling or leading you to do and spend time praying about it. Also, it is ok to talk to leaders you trust and respect about what you feel God is leading you to do.

Chapter 3 -
Go, and You Will Find

"Now there was a believer in Damascus named Ananias. The Lord spoke to him in a vision, calling, "Ananias!"

"Yes, Lord!" he replied.

[11] The Lord said, "Go over to Straight Street, to the house of Judas. When you get there, ask for a man from Tarsus named Saul. He is praying to me right now. [12] I have shown him a vision of a man named Ananias coming in and laying hands on him so he can see again." (Acts 9:10-12 NLT)

In chapter 9 of the book of Acts, we see this scene play out. God is directing Ananias to go to the house of Judas and ask for Saul. You can read the whole story in chapter 9, but Saul was not someone you wanted to play with. He was responsible for arresting many believers and even having them killed, so what God was asking Ananias to do was no simple request. It may appear so to the casual observer not familiar with the story, but it was not.

Here's what I believe was going through Ananias' mind.

God, you want me to go where and talk to who? Are you serious? Do you know who this guy is? Are you sure this is what you want me to do?

Ananias reacted no differently than you or I would have. You may have even felt this way with something you felt God was asking you to do.

The challenge when God is leading you like this is that the pieces of the puzzle don't necessarily add up in your mind. That's why faith and obedience are so important. The good news is when God leads you like this the payoff for your obedience happens a lot faster.

Let's go back to Ananias for a moment. He hears from God. He is extremely nervous and afraid, but he goes anyway. He then gets there and finds the situation exactly like God said he would. His obedience led to a payoff that confirmed what God was telling him.

When you step out to do something for God, there are times you will be terrified, nervous and even a little unsure just like Ananias.

Go anyway.

I can assure you when Ananias reached Judas' house, and he found Saul precisely the way God said he would his confidence and faith soared. What also grew was his ability to trust that he was hearing from God. God wants to do the same thing in your life.

I grew up in Brooklyn while my wife is from Barbados. Since we got married, I have been to Barbados a few times. One of the things that I find interesting and even a little humorous is the way Bajans give directions. It's a whole lot different from asking for directions in Brooklyn. They may tell you to go up the road and when you see the ackee tree on the left-hand side, and you pass the pasture and the yellow house, then make the second right turn. What they are saying is go and when you find this turn here.

Finding God's will and purpose for your life does not happen in one space of time. It is a continuous process that happens throughout the various stages of your life.

This is the same way God uses this. He tells you to go down the road. When you find this, you will know that you are moving in the right direction. He gives you confirmations along the way to teach you and to motivate you to keep going.

Jesus did this in the gospel of Matthew:

*"As they approached Jerusalem and came to Bethpage on the Mount of Olives, Jesus sent two disciples, saying to them, "***Go*** to the village ahead of you, and at once ***you will find*** a donkey tied there, with her colt by her. Untie them and bring them to me. If anyone says anything to you, say that the Lord needs them, and he will send them right away." (Matthew 21:1-3 NIV, emphasis added)*

God says I want you to go here and do this. When you get there, you are going to find this situation or scenario. When you see it, that will give you the confidence to know it is me leading you and directing your steps.

I hope you are beginning to see that finding your purpose is not a one-time event that happens in one space of time. It is an ongoing event where God continually leads you and teaches you through the various scenarios of life. God speaks, and you learn how to fine-tune your ear so you can hear him. In other words, take the burden off and enjoy the relationship. Enjoy getting to know your God. Enjoy spending time in his presence and as you do, he will lead you.

When we first got married, we used to say it's not about the destination it's about the journey. If you embrace the journey, God will use the situations of life to move you towards the destination. What I am telling you is this...go, and you will find.

Questions to consider:

Have you ever experienced a go and you will find moment?

How did you respond?

Is God speaking to you about something like this now?

Chapter 4 -
The Open-Door Confirmation

L et's consider the story of Nehemiah, who was the cupbearer to King Artaxerxes. Nehemiah was confronted with a considerable challenge because the wall of Jerusalem was torn down. He had gotten a report from Hanani and some of the other men about the Jews who had returned to Jerusalem after being in captivity in Babylon. Here's what they told him:

> *"They said to me, "Things are not going well for those who returned to the province of Judah. They are in great trouble and disgrace.*

The wall of Jerusalem has been torn down,
and the gates have been destroyed by fire."
Nehemiah 1:3 (NLT)

When Nehemiah heard this, he was greatly distressed. He wept over Jerusalem and spent several days fasting and praying. This fasting and praying led Nehemiah to pray one of the great prayers recorded in scripture. You can read the whole prayer in Nehemiah chapter 1, but I want to highlight two verses.

"The people you rescued by your great power
and strong hand are your servants. O Lord,
please hear my prayer! Listen to the prayers of
those of us who delight in honoring you.
Please grant me success today by
making the king favorable to me.
Put it into his heart to be kind to
me." (Nehemiah 1:10-11 NLT, emphasis
added)

Nehemiah wanted to go and rebuild the wall, but he wasn't sure if this was what God wanted him to do. He wanted to do this because his heart was devastated over the condition of his people. What Nehemiah needed was confirmation that he and God wanted the same thing. Since he was the cupbearer to the king, his position and responsibilities meant that he couldn't just get up and leave. You may be in a similar situation because of family, career or other pertinent obligations.

In his prayer, Nehemiah was asking God to use King Artaxerxes' favor as the signal to know that this is what you want me to do. He was saying God if you give me an open door, this will confirm what I feel you put in my heart to do. This is the reason why I call this the open-door confirmation.

Take a look at how this scenario plays out within the pages of scripture:

> *"but I replied, "Long live the king! How can I not be sad? For the city where my ancestors are buried is in ruins, and the gates have been destroyed by fire."*

The king asked, "Well, how can I help you?"

With a prayer to the God of heaven, I replied, "If it please the king, and if you are pleased with me, your servant, send me to Judah to rebuild the city where my ancestors are buried."

The king, with the queen sitting beside him, asked, "How long will you be gone? When will you return?" After I told him how long I would be gone, **the king agreed to my request.**

I also said to the king, "If it please the king, let me have letters addressed to the governors of the province west of the Euphrates River, instructing them to let me travel safely through their territories on my way to Judah. And please give me a letter addressed to Asaph, the manager of the king's forest, instructing him to give me timber. I will need it to make beams for the gates of the Temple fortress, for the city walls, and for a house for myself." **And the king granted these requests, because the gracious hand of God was on**

me." *(Nehemiah 2:3-8 NLT, emphasis added)*

There are a couple of key points to highlight about the open-door confirmation. The obvious one is that when God opened the door for Nehemiah, he opened it really wide. He not only got the blessing of the king to go, but he also got protection and provision for him to complete the task. When God leads you to do his will, he will not just open the door. He will also supply everything you need to accomplish what he wants you to do.

There is another critical point that is a little subtle. When you read chapters 1 and 2 of Nehemiah, if you read too fast, you will miss it. There were potentially 5-6 months between the time Nehemiah prayed the prayer and the opportunity came for him to make his request to the king. This is a gentle reminder that sometimes the open door will happen very quickly and

Nehemiah first prayed in the fall around November-December. He made his request in the spring around March-April.

sometimes you may have to wait. By the way, waiting doesn't mean God hasn't answered; it just means he hasn't answered yet.

That's why spending time in a relationship with God is so important. I can't stress that enough. If you pray for the open door, then wait for him to open it. It may take some time before he opens it, but when he does, you will know because his open doors swing really wide.

One last point about open doors and waiting. Waiting for God to open the door doesn't mean you don't knock on doors. Sometimes the only way to get someone to open the door is to knock on it. In Nehemiah's case, the one door he had was the king and when he presented his situation, God gave him favor. Your situation may have one door or many. You may have to knock once, or you may have to knock many times just be patient and persistent in the process. If it is God's will for you eventually the door will open.

Questions to Consider:

Have you asked God to open a door to confirm something he has put in your heart?

Are you actively knocking and patiently waiting for him to open the door?

Chapter 5 -
The Cast Your Nets Approach

There is an intriguing scene playing out in Luke chapter 5. Jesus is preaching on the shores of Galilee. The assembly of people who came to listen is so vast he begins to run out of room on the seashore to teach. They were really pressing in to hear what he had to say. I can't imagine the size of that audience but having been stuck in some big crowds, it becomes challenging to move and sometimes even breathe.

I recall when the Super Bowl was in the NYC area. We decided to go to some Super Bowl festivities that were set up in Times Square. The sea of people was so massive that it took us 45 minutes to walk one block which would typically take 45 seconds. I wonder if this was the type of scene that Jesus was encountering.

As this is happening, Jesus takes notice of two empty boats, and he asks the man who owned them if he could borrow his boat. The man agrees, so Jesus goes and sits in the boat. Jesus has the man push him out into the water, and from there he continues addressing the crowd.

The man who owned the boat was Simon also known as Peter. Jesus had two purposes. One was to instruct the crowd, but the other was to call Peter to follow him.

After teaching the multitude, Jesus told Peter, let's go fishing. Peter was an expert fisherman, and this is how he made a living. He had been fishing all night without catching anything. I can imagine Peter being tired and frustrated because he had no fish. No fish meant no money. I can relate because I used to work in commission-based sales and there were days you worked all day and didn't make a sale and no sales meant no money.

Being tired and frustrated Peter didn't want to go back out fishing at that moment. However, he relented and went out fishing for only one reason, because Jesus said so. Here is where the miracle happened. When he cast his nets again, he caught so much fish the nets started to tear. He called for help from his partners in the other boat. Even with that second boat, there was so much fish that they both began to sink.

By the time they arrived back on shore, Peter now had a full revelation and understanding of who Jesus was. Peter recognized his sinful condition and asked Jesus to leave, but Jesus used this miracle to call Peter to follow him. Jesus used the miracle to reveal his will for Peter's life. By the way, it worked because when they got back to shore, they left everything and followed Jesus.

Sometimes God will confirm what he wants you to do by asking you to cast your nets. When he asks you the response you initially give may be just like Peter. Really. Again. Don't you know I have been working on this for eight months and I haven't seen any fruit from it? I'm tired of sending out resumes. I'm tired of trying to pursue this ministry. I've pitched my idea for the last time because it seems like nobody is listening. You really want me to call that person again. You want me to pray about this one more time. When is enough, enough?

My wife Diana is a pool operator instructor. In this role, she teaches a course helping people become certified pool operators. After obtaining her instructor's license, we decided it was time for her to teach a class that she would sponsor on her own. This meant not only teaching the course but also having to fill the room. Imagine the concern over doing this because she had never done it before and there was a risk it could fail. Failing would cause us to lose money, something nobody likes doing, especially me.

God will honor obedience even if the obedience is not coming from a place of faith.

We prayed about it and felt like God was telling her to cast the nets. So that is what she did. Even though my wife was nervous and not sure of the outcome, she did it anyway. After casting the nets, the phones and requests started coming in. The more they came in, it became abundantly clear that God was with her. She was able to fill that first class. Since then she has taught more classes, and whenever she teaches one, they are always full.

God may be asking you to cast your nets. If he is, I want to be very honest with you. There will be times you won't feel like doing it. To cast your nets is scary, frustrating, and can be exhausting. Often it is done with no expectation of results. I am convinced that Peter did not believe anything was going to happen when he went out and cast the nets, but he did it anyway. This shows me that God will honor obedience even if the obedience is not coming from a place of faith.

Have you ever considered what would have happened if Peter said no? He probably would have ended up on that same shore and been just a fisherman for the rest of his life. Think of all he would have missed. It's the same thing I will say to you. Refusing to cast your nets may cause you to miss God's purpose for your life. Think about all the miracles, blessings and favor of God you could be missing because you refuse to cast your nets.

If you are honest, you may have reached a point where you don't think anything is going to happen anymore. However, could it be, that the very place God wants to lead you. The very thing he has called you to do. The very miracle God wants to work in your life. The very purpose he has created you for is tied to you doing one act of obedience…casting your nets.

I encourage you, please don't get stuck on the shore when there is so much God has for you. God's purpose for your life will often be revealed when you take steps of obedience even when you don't want to. Peter's whole life changed because he decided to cast the nets. I believe yours will too if you will be willing to cast those nets just one more time.

Questions to Consider:

Is God asking you to do something that you don't want to do anymore?

Have you given up because you are tired or frustrated?

Are you willing to obey even if you don't feel like it?

Is there a dream inside of you that you are ready to give up on?

If the answer is yes to any of these questions then I encourage you to go back to the last instruction God gave you and cast your nets and see what God will do.

Chapter 6 -
Peace in The Process

There is a beautiful hymn I remember called Wonderful Peace. Here are the lyrics to the chorus:

Peace, peace, wonderful peace,
Coming down from the Father above!
Sweep over my spirit forever, I pray
In fathomless billows of love!

Philippians 4:6-7 says,

Don't worry about anything; instead pray about everything. Tell God what you need and thank him for all he has done. If you do this, you will experience God's peace which is far more wonderful than the human mind can understand..." (NLT)

In the pursuit of God's purpose for your life sometimes you hit a snag or a fork in the road. There are decisions to be made, and you are not sure which choice is the right one. Have you ever felt this way?

You have two job offers which one do you take?

You feel like you should move and you visited this city, but you are not sure if you should move there.

You believe God wants you to step out into this ministry, but you are so nervous about taking the first step.

You feel like this is the person you should marry yet you don't want to make the wrong decision.

Situations like these are not only common, but they are the types of scenarios you will face many times as you go through this journey called life. In these situations, often the thing that God will lead you with is his peace.

God's peace is often most noticeable when there is chaos all around you.

We were living in Queens and wanted to leave NYC for a more "suburban" lifestyle. One of our requirements in moving was we didn't want to live too far away from NYC because of our relationship with family, friends and at that time church. We didn't know where we wanted to go, but we started looking. We eventually made our way to Connecticut and moved to a town where we didn't know anyone. All we had to guide us was the peace of God in knowing we were making the right decision for our family.

Here is an interesting thing about God's peace. It doesn't always match the specific circumstance you are facing. While there are many times that it will, there will however be situations that may be chaotic, and yet you walk into it because you have God's peace. In many instances, God's peace becomes the assurance that you are in the place you need to be regardless of how it looks on the outside. By the way, peace doesn't mean you know the outcome, or the endpoint it just means you are sure you are walking in the right direction.

To further update our moving story. Since we moved, we have benefited from better educational opportunities for our children — better services for our son with special needs. God has also increased our capacity to serve and helped us create a ministry platform to impact the body of Christ. We moved with God's peace in our hearts, and now we are certain we are in the place God wants us to be.

Philippians tells us the way we get to this place of peace is through prayer. There it is again. Do you see it? I hope you have caught on by now and have been paying attention to the common thread that is evident through this whole process of finding God's will. You must be in a relationship with God and prayer is a critical element to that relationship. The primary goal in writing this book is not to make this pursuit of discovering God's will some mystical journey where God is dangling this carrot before you that you will never grab. No this is about understanding that the more you spend time with God. The more you commune with him. The more you get to know his voice. The more time you spend in His word, the more he will reveal to you and the easier it will become to decipher his will and purpose. In other words, you can't pursue God's purpose without pursuing God in the process.

> *You can't pursue God's purpose without pursuing God in the process.*

As you continue to pursue him, one of the things he will use to guide you is his peace. If you have ever seen an enormous ocean liner or cruise ship, they are steered by a relatively small rudder. When the ship needs to turn it doesn't make hard left or right turns like you would in a car. There aren't big, sweeping, aggressive movements but a more subtle, gentle turning as the captain positions the rudder in the direction he wants the ship to go.

I remember a time when I was faced with a decision about an opportunity I was considering. After having an initial conversation with the gentleman about it everything seemed like it would be a go. However, in my spirit I couldn't find the peace of God giving me clearance to pursue this opportunity. Everything on the surface seemed great but I was missing the peace of God in my heart. For this reason, I turned down the opportunity.

This is how God uses peace in your life. His peace will be the rudder. He will gently steer you with it. He will steer you away from what he doesn't want in your life and into the purpose he has for you. Peace, peace what wonderful peace.

Chapter 7 -

The Still Small Voice

---

¹¹ Then He said, "Go out, and stand on the mountain before the Lord." And behold, the Lord passed by, and a great and strong wind tore into the mountains and broke the rocks in pieces before the Lord, but the Lord was not in the wind; and after the wind an earthquake, but the Lord was not in the earthquake; ¹² and after the earthquake a fire, but the Lord was not in the fire; and after the fire a still small voice.

¹³ So it was, when Elijah heard it, that he wrapped his face in his mantle and went out and stood in the entrance of the cave. Suddenly

a voice came to him, and said, "What are you doing here, Elijah?" —(1 Kings 19:11-13 NKJV)

I happen to be a big fan of pro wrestling. Please no emails telling me don't you know its fake. I know it is sports entertainment. One of my favorite wrestlers of all time is Ric Flair. One of the things that made Flair great was his ring entrance. It started with loud music booming through the sound system. Smoke would fill the entranceway where he would appear. Usually his match was the biggest match of the night and was often the main event. There was always a buzz in the crowd as they waited for Flair to make this grand entrance. They were creating an expectation that something great and exciting was about to happen, something you didn't want to miss. After a while, once the anticipation had built up Ric Flair would appear with his expensive sequined robe and eventually make his walk down the aisle to the ring. The crowd would erupt and eventually you would get a trademark Ric Flair wooooo.

So often this is the expectation that we have when we are looking for God's will. We want the big dramatic moment, coupled with the voice from heaven or the dramatic laying on of hands and God declaring from heaven "this is my son/daughter in whom I am well pleased. Go and do this thing I have assigned for you."

As you have probably experienced, that is the exception and not the rule of how God leads you. It's great when he does lead that way but it doesn't happen often and when it does it's usually when you are least expecting it. If you look at Elijah, we discover that God often does something very different and not as dramatic. (He didn't speak through the hurricane or earthquake) He chose to speak in a gentle whisper or a still small voice. When compared to Elijah you have one great advantage that Elijah didn't have, the Spirit of God dwells within you. Jesus said in John 14:16-17

And I will ask the Father, and he will give you another Advocate, who will never leave you. He is the Holy Spirit, who leads into all truth. The world cannot receive him, because it isn't looking for him and doesn't recognize him. But you know him, because he lives with you now and later will be in you. (NLT)

Though the Holy Spirit is God and is all powerful, one of the images we see of Him is a dove. Gentle and peaceful. Though he could be forceful and barge in, he often doesn't. When God is speaking to you through the Holy Spirit, he will often whisper quiet words to your spirit gently leading or moving you into the direction he wants you to move in. This is another reason why spending time with God is so important. Doing so allows you get to know and understand those gentle leadings and nudgings that the Holy Spirit gives you.

When I was in college, I used to deliver newspapers very early in the morning. I would start around 3 am and usually by 6 am I would be finished. One day when delivering the papers, I had to go into an apartment building. I felt this impression in my heart, very gently, don't take the elevator walk up the stairs. I decided not to listen as I said it's not that big of a deal and I didn't feel like walking up to the 4th floor.

Ignoring the prompting, I got on the elevator, and we made it up to the 4th floor. The elevator, however, stopped a little short of the floor and I had to take a small step up to get out. After I stepped out, I delivered the newspapers I had and was ready to go back downstairs. Again, I felt that gentle whisper, don't get in the elevator take the stairs. I decided to ignore that whisper and got back in the elevator to go downstairs. This time the elevator stopped short of the floor, the door would not open, and I was stuck. Oh, did I mention it was 5 am on a Sunday, and no one was getting up early to go to work. Also, there was no alarm in the elevator (this tells you how long ago this was). For the younger generation, I couldn't use my cell phone not because I couldn't get a signal but because they hadn't been created yet. I probably stayed in that elevator about 2 hours before someone came by and I was able to let them know I was stuck. They called the fire department, and they eventually got me out after about 3 hours being in that elevator. All of this because I chose to ignore that gentle whisper and prompting of the Holy Spirit in my heart.

When God is leading you and ordering your steps, I would say most of the time, this is how he does it. Your responsibility is to tune your ear, so you know when The Holy Spirit is whispering to you. Jesus said my sheep hear my voice, I know them, and they follow me.

So, I ask you, how will you get to know Jesus' voice? You have to spend time with him. I have a wife and two kids. I could be anywhere in a room, and if any of them open their mouths and speak, I will know who it is. I don't even have to be looking. I recognize their voice because I have been around them so much. This is the same requirement of you and Jesus. Spend so much time with Him that when the Holy Spirit whispers to you to move in a direction, regardless of where you are you will know that voice and be able to respond accordingly. The voice may not come in the earthquake, so be ready to listen for the still small voice.

Questions to Consider:

Has God been speaking gently to your heart about something he wants you to do?

Have you been spending time trying to hear and learn God's voice?

Practical Application: A good way to know God's voice is to know his word. God's word is his voice and often when he speaks he will remind you of what he has already said in his word.

Chapter 8 -
Third Party Confirmation

I n Isaiah 38 King Hezekiah became deathly ill. He was told by the prophet Isaiah he would not recover. He was going to die. In response to this Hezekiah cried out to the Lord earnestly and the Bible says after praying he broke down and wept bitterly. Here is the prayer Hezekiah prayed:

> *"Remember, O Lord, how I have always been faithful to you and have served you single-mindedly, always doing what pleases you." –* (Isaiah 38:3 NLT)

Hezekiah was pouring his heart out before the Lord because he did not want to die at that time. After Hezekiah's prayer God responded by giving this message to the prophet Isaiah to deliver to Hezekiah:

"This is what the Lord, the God of your ancestor David says, I have heard your prayer and seen your tears. I will add fifteen years to your life." - (Isaiah 38:5 NLT)

Let's analyze deeper what happened here.

Hezekiah in his distress pours his heart out before God and is in desperate need of an answer from God. God seeing his prayer delivers the message through Isaiah. God used someone else, a third party, to confirm what Hezekiah had been praying for in secret.

Can you relate to this?

Are there secret questions or decisions in your heart that you are pouring out before God?

You believe God is moving you in a particular direction, yet you haven't told anyone. You are still a little unsure if this is the step to take. Then what seems like out of the blue you begin getting confirmations from all over the place of what God has put in your heart to do. You may get a phone call from a friend who encourages you to move in this direction. You go to church, and the pastor preaches right to your situation as if he had just spoken with you. Or someone prays for you, and they pray the exact thing that was in your heart which you never told them about. These are all examples of third-party confirmation.

A few years ago, my wife and I felt that God was leading us to leave the church we had been attending. I had been there for seven years and my wife for three years. We knew it was time to leave, but we didn't know where to go. When we finally left the church, I remember the

> By the way in case you're wondering we didn't go to separate churches for four years. She came to my church after we started dating and got married.

first Sunday we woke up without a home church. It felt weird like we were orphans. We decided to start visiting a few churches in the area. We went to one in particular that a few of our friends attended. Even though the services were excellent, we didn't sense that this is the place God wanted us.

One week we decided that the following Sunday we would go to my wife's old church in The Bronx, we were living in Queens at the time. She had always told me how awesome the music was and the incredible worship that she experienced. Because of the way she spoke about the church it created in me a genuine excitement about going.

During that week however, something happened. In my heart, I got a strong impression from the Holy Spirit that we should visit a different church. This church was one my sister had recommended, because she thought we would like it. The impression I received was so strong that I immediately told my wife we are going to change plans and go to this church on Sunday.

A little while later I got a phone call from a friend who used to attend the church we had just left. That might seem ordinary but having him call me was unusual. In the seven years I had known him, I can count on one hand the number of times he had called me, or we had even spoken on the phone. What makes this more interesting is the reason he was calling. The reason for the phone call was that he was attending a new church and wanted to invite me to attend this Sunday. I know that doesn't sound like much, but as God would have it, the new church he asked me to visit was the same church my sister had recommended. This was also the same one God impressed upon my heart to visit.

God put it on his heart to call us. God used a disconnected third party, who didn't even know we were looking for a church. I'm sure he was completely unaware of the process we were in, and he didn't realize we had left our old church. God used him to confirm that this was what he wanted us to do. In case you were wondering, we never made it to my wife's old church.

Third-party confirmations can come from a variety of places. In our case, it was a friend. However, it could be a message, a song, a conversation, a sermon or even a prayer. Regardless of how it comes, there are two things to remember about it. First, you don't go looking for it; God brings it to you. That's what happened to Hezekiah, and that's what happened to us. Second, the confirmation is of something that God has already placed in your heart. Hezekiah's was an answer to a specific prayer. Ours was a confirmation of a particular instruction. When these two things line up, then you can move with a level of confidence knowing that God is confirming what he wants you to do.

Chapter 9 -
The Disturbia Effect

In the book of Esther, you will find the story of Queen Esther. One of the central characters in the story is a man named Haman. This man had a disdain for the Jews living in the Persian kingdom. At this time the kingdom was led by King Xerxes.

This disdain, which was mainly fueled by a perceived disrespect by a gentleman named Mordecai, led him to devise a plot to eliminate all the Jews. Esther was the queen, Mordecai was her uncle, and they were both Jewish. In this great plan created by Haman all the Jews throughout the kingdom, which stretched from India to Ethiopia, would be killed on the same day. Mordecai reaches out to Esther asking her to go before the king to request that he put a stop to this plan. Esther replies to Mordecai stating I can't just walk in to see the king without an invitation. If I do that I will be killed. Here is how Mordecai responded to her,

> 13 *Mordecai sent this reply to Esther: "Don't think for a moment that because you're in the palace, you will escape when all other Jews are killed.* 14 *If you keep quiet at a time like this, deliverance and relief for the Jews will arise from some other place, but you and your relatives will die. Who knows if perhaps you were made queen for just such a time as this?"* *(Esther 4:13-14 NLT)*

After receiving this message, this was Esther's response,

> 15 *Then Esther sent this reply to Mordecai:* 16 *"Go and gather together all the Jews of Susa and fast for me. Do not eat or drink for*

three days, night or day. My maids and I will do the same. And then, though it is against the law, I will go in to see the king. If I must die, I must die." (Esther 4:15-16 NLT)

Many times, God uses trouble to get you to take action and to move you into his plan. I have labeled this trouble the Disturbia Effect. We don't often view difficulty in this way, yet it is one of the ways God uses to get our attention. Esther is unique because she was in position to help, but she was initially afraid to assist. It took Mordecai to upset the apple cart to get her to take some action. The action she took spared the lives of all the Jews in the kingdom.

In 2012 I had been working at my previous employer for 12 years. I was getting to the point where I wanted to leave, but I said let me stay just one more year. On Monday, July 16 of that year, we had a conference call with about 100 people on the phone. On the call, they said as of

> *God will often use trouble to get you to take action and move.*

Friday you will no longer be employed here. Everyone on the phone was stunned, including me. You could hear some people crying in shock. I distinctly remember one lady with a tearful tremor in her voice mentioning she was seven months pregnant what was she going to do. Needless to say this created Disturbia. To add to it I was married about seven months at the time, have a son with special needs and would soon discover we were about to have another child.

Upon getting news of this kind I did what everyone may want to do in that situation. I went to Disney World. My family had already planned a trip and we weren't sure if we could go but after I got that news we decided to go.

Amid all of this "Disturbia," there was a blessing on the other side. God used it to open a different door and opportunity that

I would have never even considered had he not troubled the waters. There was a position and opportunity that God had for me, but I was somewhat comfortable where I was and not ready to move. God used this situation to get me moving causing me to take action. These actions allowed him to propel me to the place he wanted me to be.

Has God ever troubled waters in your life?

God will do this from time to time not because he wants to hurt you but because he knows if he doesn't, you will never move forward.

It's like taking the training wheels off when learning to ride a bike. It feels scary and uncomfortable, but if you don't, you'll never learn to ride correctly. You will be stuck with them for the rest of your life.

The Disturbia Effect is about God doing what he has to do to get you out of your comfort zone. Sometimes the most dangerous and unproductive place in your life is in the comfort zone. When you are in the comfort zone, you can become lazy, unmotivated and ultimately unproductive. I can assure you this is not God's purpose for you. God is all about progress and forward mobility. When you stop moving forward, he has to get you back in motion. To accomplish this, he may have to create or allow Disturbia.

Disturbia could be the loss of a job or missing a promotion. A relationship that suddenly ends. It could come in the form of a sudden illness or a business deal that goes bad. This list can go on and on, but the result is still the same. God desires to move you into the purpose he has for you.

Are you facing Disturbia in your life right now? Have you been hit with a situation that makes you feel like what in the world is going on?

If you are, I would like you to consider for a moment that God may be creating a scenario to move you. He is not looking to punish you but may be looking to promote you. He is not looking to hurt you but to bless you. So, before you cast out the situation. Before you rebuke the devil or try to pray it away. Before you automatically dismiss it as an attack. I want you to do something different. Embrace it. That's right embrace the Disturbia with the proper perspective. Discover if God is doing something different amid the turmoil. See if there is a place, posture or position he wants you to take in the middle of your situation. Doing this will bring about the good that God has planned for your life.

As difficult and challenging as it can be the Disturbia may be the next step in your journey. The thing God will use to help you get to the incredible plan that he has designed for you. I am not saying that this will always feel good, but if you embrace it, the end will be good.

Questions to Consider:

Are you facing a Disturbia situation in your life?

Are you embracing it or trying to fight it?

Ask God what position does he want you to take in the midst of this Disturbia?

Chapter 10 -
Signs and Wonders

The story of Gideon begins in the book of Judges chapter 6. During this time the Israelites were being oppressed by the Midianites, and the Midianites were ruthless. They were a group of people that were strong and forceful. They took everything from the Israelites and didn't leave them anything. If the Israelites had it and the Midianites saw it, they seized it. They were beyond aggressive. I would say down-right nasty.

The reason Israel was facing oppression was because they chose to do evil in God's eyes and would not repent. Because of their choice God decided to hand them over to the Midianites. Over time Israel reached a point where they had had enough. When the weight of their oppression became too great and they got tired of being abused by the Midianites they finally decided to call on God. In their fatigue, they cried out to God for help, and God responded.

Here is where we are introduced to Gideon. We find Gideon threshing wheat in the bottom of a winepress so he could hide it from the Midianites. He did this because he afraid. He knew if they found out he had wheat they would take it. In the middle of his hiding an angel of the Lord shows up. He tells Gideon that he is going to be the one God will use to bring deliverance from the Midianites. Here's what happened next.

14 Then the Lord turned to him and said, "Go with the strength you have, and rescue Israel from the Midianites. I am sending you!"

¹⁵ *"But Lord," Gideon replied, "how can I rescue Israel? My clan is the weakest in the whole tribe of Manasseh, and I am the least in my entire family!"*

¹⁶ *The Lord said to him, "I will be with you. And you will destroy the Midianites as if you were fighting against one man."*

¹⁷ *Gideon replied, "If you are truly going to help me,* **show me a sign** *to prove that it is really the Lord speaking to me. (NLT, emphasis added)*

Gideon was overwhelmed by what God wanted him to do. Especially considering how powerful the Midianites were. Looking at himself, he couldn't figure out how he, little old Gideon, was going to defeat the mighty and ruthless Midianites. Because this seemed outrageous, out of the norm and probably in Gideon's mind downright crazy, he asked God for a sign. Gideon asked three times before he was convinced. The first sign in vs. 17 was to confirm it was the Lord speaking to him. The other signs in vs. 36-40 were to confirm God was going to be with him. I guess the third sign was the charm because after that Gideon moved to do what God told him.

Has God ever approached you with a "Gideon-like" situation?

Has God ever asked you to do something that to you seems crazy or even impossible?

In these moments your natural response and instinct could possibly be a lot like Gideon's. You may ask,

God, is this you?

Are you sure this is what you want me to do?

God do you know who I am?

How will I ever be able to do that?

I believe in situations like these where the thing God is asking you to do may seem way over the top it can be appropriate to ask God for a sign. Should you do this make sure you are not asking because of unbelief but because the thing God is asking you to do goes beyond your imagination. The thing may feel so great you need some Godly encouragement. Gideon was asking because he was afraid and before he went running into battle against the powerful Midianites, he wanted some reassurance. His reassurance and encouragement came by asking God for a sign.

Even though asking for a sign from God may be appropriate in some instances. I want to caution you about always looking for them or always needing them. Most of the time that is not how God works. If you're not careful it can lead to deception. Many people have been deceived because they went looking for a sign.

Here are three things to be mindful of:

1. If you look for signs, you can find them so be careful when asking. You can turn almost anything into a sign.

2. Make sure you're asking because you want to obey not because you want an excuse to disobey.

3. Sometimes people get ridiculous in asking for signs. I heard a lady say once, "God if you want me to do this then when I wake up tomorrow let the sun be red and the sky yellow, and I will know it's you." Not only is this ridiculous, I believe this mindset is coming from a heart that doesn't want to obey God.

Here's the bottom line about signs and wonders. Does God use them? Yes. Does God use them all the time? No. However, if you ask God for one make sure it is coming from the right heart and right mindset. You desire to obey. You just want confirmation and encouragement that you are following the voice of God and no one else.

Chapter 11 -
The Dream Factor

There are various places throughout scripture where God has used dreams to make his intentions known to men. You will see this in both the Old and New Testament. In one instance in Matthew 2 we discover the story of the wise men. In this scenario, the wise men were following a star in the east which was leading them to Jesus. They were looking for this newborn King Jesus because they wanted to worship him. After a conversation with Herod, they made their way to Bethlehem. Herod told the wise men when you find him, please come back and let me know so I may worship him as well. He had no desire to worship Jesus but was hoping to find him and kill him. Here's what happened after that:

> *⁹ After this interview the wise men went their way. And the star they had seen in the east guided them to Bethlehem. It went ahead of them and stopped over the place where the child was. ¹⁰ When they saw the star, they were filled with joy! ¹¹ They entered the house and saw the child with his mother, Mary, and they bowed down and worshiped him. Then they opened their treasure chests and gave him gifts of gold, frankincense, and myrrh.*
>
> *¹² When it was time to leave, they returned to their own country by another route,* **for God had warned them in a dream not to return to Herod.** *– (Matthew 2:9-12 NLT, emphasis added)*

In an earlier chapter, I told you the story of a friend who had recently passed away. He felt compelled by God to change his schedule and return home earlier than planned. What I left out was how God revealed this to him. After he decided to stay and not go back, he chose to pray about that decision. As he was praying, God kept showing him a big red sign and a clear message in his heart indicating you must get on that plane. As you know in the story, his presence on that plane saved a man's life. Here is how the story all ties together. As the medical personnel was wheeling the man down the aisle, my friend looked, and the man was wearing some big red sneakers. He was able to connect the dots, and he knew then God had spoken to him.

Just as he did with the wise men and just as he did with my friend God will sometimes use dreams to lead you and direct you. This does not mean that every dream you have is from the Lord. Some may be but honestly most will not be. You cannot, however, discount that God will use this as a means of speaking to you. There is one key indicator that God is directing you in a dream. The dream will often come with instruction or some movement to action. The dream you have when you are asleep is often accompanied by a strong desire to respond when you are awake. When we look at the wise men, God used the dream to warn them, and this caused them to return home another way. In my friend's case, God stirred his heart to have him rearrange his trip and go back earlier.

I know some people may read this and consider this to be a little farfetched but let me assure you it's not. God is the same yesterday, today and forever. Malachi 3:6 says, *"I am the Lord, and I do not change..."*. (NLT)

If God did it then, he can do it now. It may not be the way he always uses. However, don't be surprised if he does.

Chapter 12 -
The Safety of Counsel

The way of a fool seems right to them, but the wise listen to advice. — (Proverbs 12:15 NIV)

Plans fail for lack of counsel, but with many advisers they succeed. — (Proverbs 15:22 NIV)

When you reach the point where you feel a degree of confidence that God is leading you in a particular direction, then it's time to do what Proverbs says. Get counsel. Seek advice.

God has put trusted leaders and other people around you to help you decipher what God is saying to you. The purpose of counsel is not so they can tell you what God wants you to do. They are there to ensure that your process of decision making is sound and biblical. This is especially necessary when the decisions you make involve a change of location, change of job, career or ministry. It is also critical when there are children, spouses or family situations affected by the decision you make.

When I decided to marry Diana that decision didn't just impact my life. I was bringing a son with me. I had to be sure that God was leading me in this because I could not afford to be wrong. If I got it wrong, it wouldn't just be bad for me. It would be bad for my son as well. Knowing this I made sure to follow the advice of Proverbs. I spoke to my pastor, and other men who I knew were godly men. I knew I could trust these men and that they would tell me the truth.

Those are critical elements of the counsel you should seek. Make sure they are godly, which means they follow biblical principles as a way of life. Also, make sure they will tell you the truth. It also helps if you have some level of relationship with them.

When you are trying to accomplish God's will you want people around you full of the wisdom that comes from God's word and the Holy Spirit. You also want people that will point out some red flags should they pop up when you talk about your decision-making process.

Choosing to follow God's will should not just flow out of your unchecked whims and impulses. Does God lead that way? Yes, sometimes. There will be times when that can happen, but usually, that is the exception, not the rule. For the most part, deciphering God's will follow a biblical and rational decision-making process. It is not

> *God never intended for you to discover his purpose for your life in a vacuum. That's why you need the body of Christ.*

a requirement, but it is usually part of the process. That's why you should be able to explain your decision-making process to people you trust. That's why counsel matters.

This process is not about you being a lone ranger. That is a dangerous person to be. God never intended for you to discover his purpose for your life in a vacuum. That's why you are part of a church. That's why you are surrounded by godly brothers and sisters in Christ. That's why he put you in the Body of Christ. If none of these things exist in your life right now, then that's your first step. Find a trustworthy, true, bible-believing church and get connected to the Body of Christ. People who feel they don't need to be part of a local church or fellowship with the Body of Christ will have a challenging time discovering God's plan for their life. Proverbs will call that person a fool.

As I close this chapter know that you should be able to trust the people and leadership God has placed around you. You should not be afraid to speak to them to get counsel. Those people are there to help you grow in your walk and to help you discover all the great things God has in store for your life.

The Conclusion

As we come to the end of our
conversation, I want to reiterate what I
said at the very beginning. By the time we
are finished, you will have a greater
understanding of God's will and purpose
for you. You will know the different ways
God leads you into his purpose. In other
words, you will know what to look for.

I pray these words have given you greater
insight and ultimately greater desire to
pursue the excellent plan God has for you.
One final thought. Don't stress over
trying to figure out the plan. I know that
sounds weird in a book about finding
God's purpose. However, instead of
stressing, spend your time experiencing the
joy that comes from building your
relationship with Jesus. This is the most

important thing. I can assure you if you get this right then God will certainly make sure you get the rest of it right.

Remember, you can't pursue God's plan without pursuing God. For this reason, I encourage you to spend lots of time drawing near to God. As you draw near to him, he has promised he will draw near to you. When you do this, he will order and direct your steps. He will take the responsibility to lead you into this wonderful plan he has for your life. The good news is now you know some of the ways he will do it.

As we move from here, I am excited about all the awesome things God is going to do in your life. Remember this. The most essential ability God will use in your life is availability. Make yourself available and watch what he will do. I pray God's grace and peace as you pursue his purpose for your life.

The Invitation

Throughout this book I have spent a great deal of time referring to this wonderful plan God has for your life. Here's the first step in the plan. God wants to have a personal relationship with you. I believe the whole course of your life hinges on how you respond to this desire. In my view this is the most important decision you will ever make in your life.

If it's so important it begs the question, how do you begin this relationship? The answer is surprisingly simple. Because God loves you so deeply, he made a provision for this relationship to be possible. God sent his son Jesus to die for your sins. He offers you the opportunity to have all your sins forgiven. The slate of your life can be wiped clean and you can have a new beginning. This beginning will transform your life and put you on the path to become everything God created you to be.

This new relationship can begin when you receive Jesus as your personal savior. It's not hard. You can pray this prayer. When you pray believe it with all your heart and you will be saved.

Dear Jesus,

Today I confess my sins and I believe you are Lord. I ask you today to forgive my sins, come into my heart and lead me into the perfect plan you have for me.

That's it! I told you it was simple. If you have prayed that with all sincerity, then congratulations. You are now part of God's family. Would you please do one thing for me?

Please send an email to hello@thebiblestudyclub.com and let me know you have made this decision. I want to rejoice with you and help you take the next steps in your journey.

About the Author

Clarence L. Haynes Jr. is first and foremost a husband and father which after his relationship with Jesus Christ is his most important ministry of all. Outside of that he is a rising speaker, teacher, author and co-founder of The Bible Study Club. The club was founded in 2018 and was formed to create a platform where anyone could come and learn God's word in a live, online format. Clarence and his wife Diana have a passion to serve the body of Christ and help believers become everything God has destined for them to become.

For more information about their ministry please visit www.thebiblestudyclub.com or www.clarencehaynes.com

Additional Resources

As a special thank you for purchasing this book we would like to give you a free copy of an e-book called

5 Daily Practices to Help You Renew Your Mind.

Please visit www.thebiblestudyclub.com and download a free copy.

Made in the USA
Middletown, DE
17 September 2021